DISCOVERIES That Changed the World

CURIOUS Questions and Answers

DISCOVERIES That Changed the World

CURIOUS Questions and Answers

Words by Simon Adams, Anna Claybourne, Sue Nicholson and Robert Snedden

Illustrations by Fabrizio di Baldo, Elissambura, Pauline Gregory, Flavio Remonetti and Steve Wood (cover)

Miles Kelly

First published in 2024 by Miles Kelly Publishing Ltd
Harding's Barn, Bardfield End Green, Thaxted, Essex, CM6 3PX, UK
Unit 5A The Court, Ashbourne Industrial Estate, Ashbourne,
Co. Meath, A84 DP73, Eire

Copyright © Miles Kelly Publishing Ltd 2024

2 4 6 8 10 9 7 5 3

Publishing Directors   Belinda Gallagher, Fran Bromage
Creative Director   Jo Cowan
Editorial Director   Rosie Neave
Managing Editor   Amy Johnson
Senior Editors   Becky Miles, Ruth Redford
Designers   Joe Jones, Simon Lee, Andrea Slane, Karen Doughty, Venita Kidwai
Image Manager   Liberty Newton
Production   Elizabeth Collins
Reprographics   Stephan Davis

All rights reserved. No part of this publication may be reproduced, stored in a retrieval system, or transmitted by any means, electronic, mechanical, photocopying, recording or otherwise, without the prior permission of the copyright holder.

ISBN 978-1-78989-839-2

Printed in China

British Library Cataloguing-in-Publication Data
A catalogue record for this book is available
from the British Library

Made with paper from a sustainable forest

www.mileskelly.net

CONTENTS

EPIC EXPLORERS   10

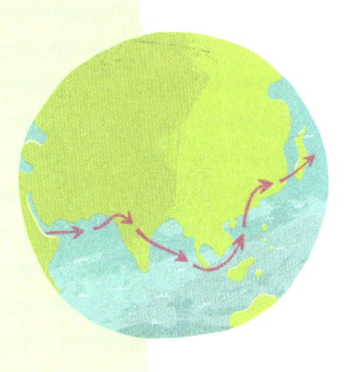

INCREDIBLE JOURNEYS   42

CLEVER INVENTORS   74

SUPER SCIENTISTS   106

Index   138

EPIC EXPLORERS

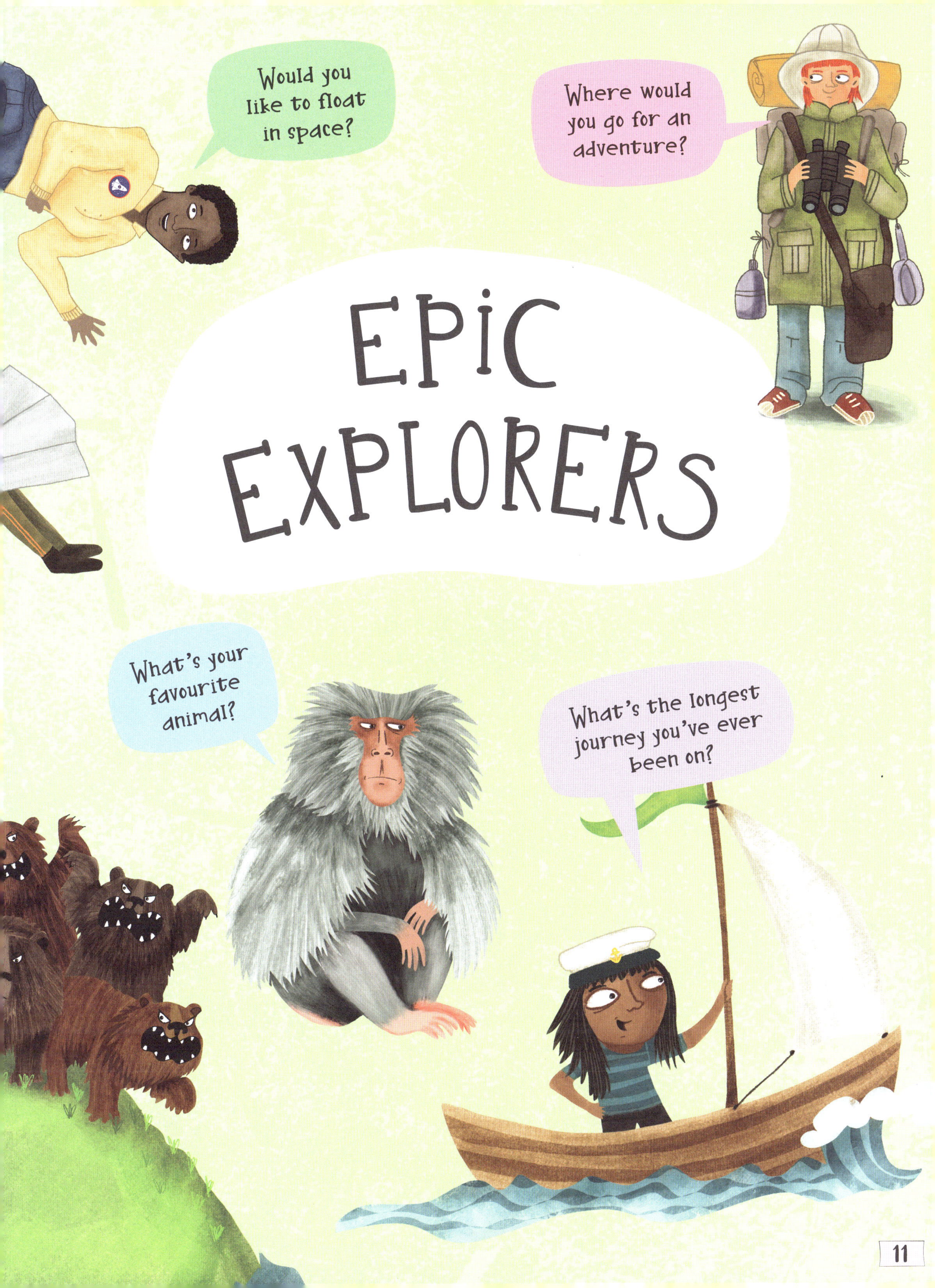

Would you like to float in space?

Where would you go for an adventure?

What's your favourite animal?

What's the longest journey you've ever been on?

When did people start exploring?

The first people lived in Africa and began to explore the rest of the world about 200,000 years ago. By 10,000 years ago humans had settled in most parts of the world.

Are we there yet?

Which queen found a magical land?

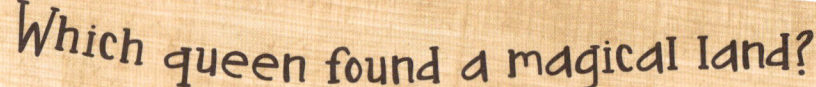

In around 1490 BCE **Queen Hatshepsut** of ancient Egypt sent ships across the Red Sea to find new people to trade with. They reached a land called Punt (probably Somalia in East Africa) and returned with precious things never seen before.

The Egyptians brought me back from Punt, but weren't sure what sort of animal I was.

Baboon

Who brought back tales of the midnight Sun?

In around 320 BCE, the Greek sailor **Pytheas** headed north from the Mediterranean. He saw the frozen Arctic Ocean, and described a land where the Sun never set in summer.

Why is it so light at night?

Who crossed a vast ocean without maps?

Polynesian people did, from around 3600 years ago. They followed the Sun and stars, looked at the clouds, waves and wind direction, and found new islands to live on across the Pacific Ocean.

Follow that bird!

I visited far eastern lands where hardly anyone from Europe had ever been.

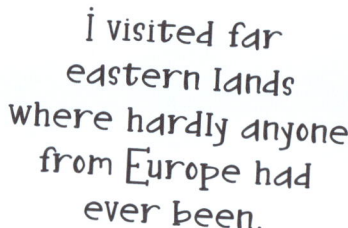

Was the Silk Road made of silk?

No – it was named for the Chinese silk that was carried along it to be traded in Europe. In 1271, Italian merchant **Marco Polo** travelled the Silk Road route from Venice to China.

I travelled all over China and Asia and became super-famous when I wrote the story of my travels.

How did ice cream get to Italy?

Some people say the idea was brought back by **Marco Polo** after he learnt about similar desserts on his travels in China.

Did you know?

Say cheese!

British Victorian explorer **Isabella Bird** was also a talented photographer who recorded tales of her travels that amazed the public back at home.

I thought you'd be cuter!

On a trip to Sumatra in 1292, **Marco Polo** was on the hunt for unicorns. Instead, he saw a rhinoceros, and thought he had found one.

American explorer **Hiram Bingham** brought the forgotten Inca city of Machu Picchu in the Andes mountains to world attention in 1911.

I campaigned for womens' rights and climbed mountains into my eighties.

American mountaineer **Annie Smith Peck** placed a flag that said 'Votes for Women' on the top of Mount Coropuna in Peru in 1911.

British explorer **Gertrude Bell** helped to create the state of Iraq in 1921 after the collapse of the Ottoman Empire.

i advised governments, set up museums, and helped draw the map of Iraq.

Alaska's Admiralty Island is home to lots of grizzly bears. It's known as **'Fortress of the Bears'** in the local Tlingit language, and early Russian explorers called it 'Fear Island'!

English explorer **Mary Kingsley** bravely travelled alone through West Africa in the 1890s. She fought crocodiles and had three new species of fish named after her.

Mount Disappointment in Australia got its name when two British explorers climbed to the top in 1824 and couldn't see the sea!

17

Why isn't Greenland green?

Because the Viking sailor **Erik the Red** lied about it! Erik travelled to the island around 1000 CE. He found it cold and icy, but named it Greenland to try to get more people to join him.

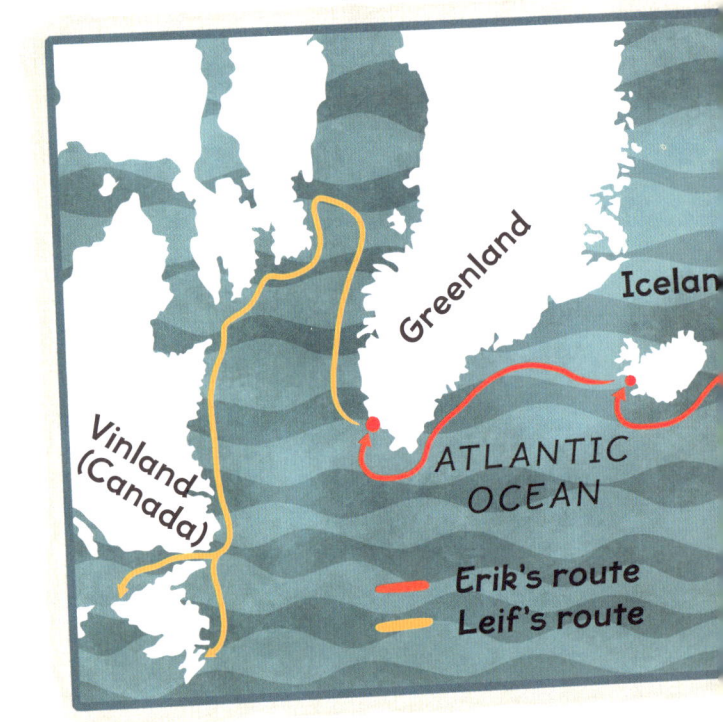

Wow, it's SO GREEN here!

Erm... really?

Who visited America but didn't stay?

Erik the Red's son, **Leif Erikson**, and his fellow Vikings explored a place he called Vinland, in modern-day Canada. They founded a new settlement but didn't stay very long before returning to Greenland.

Where did Columbus think he was?

When Italian explorer **Christopher Columbus** landed on an island he named San Salvador in 1492, he thought it was part of Asia. In fact, it was the Bahamas, and he was actually on the continent now called America.

How wonderful to be in Asia!

Asia? No, buddy, you should have turned left at Africa.

What was the Age of Exploration?

Europeans started to sail great distances around the globe from the 1480s, in a time we call the Age of Exploration. They made new trade routes and claimed foreign lands.

Vasco da Gama

Who made it easier to get spices?

Portuguese explorer **Vasco da Gama** did when he found a new sea route to India in 1498.

Before then, spices from India and the Far East used to take ages to get to Europe over land.

So, da Gama's discovery made the spice journey much easier.

Who first sailed all around the world?

In 1522, **Juan Sebastián Elcano** returned to Spain after a three-year journey around the globe. He was part of explorer **Ferdinand Magellan**'s expedition to find a route west to far eastern Spice Islands. He led the voyage after Magellan died in 1521.

Juan Sebastián Elcano

How did Canada get its name?

In 1535, **Jacques Cartier** sailed to north America from France. The local Iroquois people gave him directions to a village, which they called a kanata. Cartier thought the whole region was called kanata, which evolved into the name 'Canada'.

The kanata is that way.

Ah, I see — we're in Canada!

- Magellan's route
- da Gama's route
- Cartier's route

NORTH AMERICA
ATLANTIC OCEAN
EUROPE
AFRICA
ASIA
PACIFIC OCEAN
SOUTH AMERICA
OCEANIA

Magellan died here

Ferdinand Magellan

After getting past the wild tip of South America we found a vast, calm sea, which I named the Pacific Ocean.

Many explorers came home with great riches, but they often caused a lot of damage, spreading deadly diseases. The new sea routes also led to the start of the terrible transatlantic slave trade.

How many?

37 — The distance in metres of the first plane flight, by **Orville Wright** in 1903. That's shorter than the wingspan of a jumbo jet!

72 — The record-breaking number of days it took American **Nellie Bly** to travel all around the world in 1889 — before planes were invented.

I proved women could break travel records at a time when many people expected us to stay at home.

12 — The number of people to have ever walked on the Moon.

£7 million — The amount of gold captured by English explorer **Francis Drake** from a Spanish ship in 1578.

400,000 — The number of people estimated by NASA who worked to get them there!

19

The time in days it took British pilot **Amy Johnson** to fly solo from England to Australia in 1930, becoming the first woman to do so.

It's a bit cold up here! Shall we go?

15

The time in minutes spent on the summit of Mount Everest by **Edmund Hillary** and **Tenzing Norgay**, the first people to climb it in 1953.

I sailed around the world twice, and also walked and rode over 32,000 kilometres.

240,000

The distance in kilometres sailed by one of the first female explorers, Austrian **Ida Pfeiffer**, on her travels in the 1840s and 1850s.

23.7 billion

Distance in kilometres from Earth of the Voyager 1 space probe, which has been exploring the Solar System for 44 years and counting!

Who sailed in a coal boat?

British explorer **James Cook** was chosen to captain a former coal boat, the *Endeavour*, on a journey around the world in 1768. He made two further global voyages, exploring many places that hadn't been mapped.

Cook visited Australia, New Zealand, Tahiti, Hawaii, and even got close to Antarctica, mapping many coastlines along the way.

> I grew up sailing coal boats off the Yorkshire coast, so I knew she was the ship for me!

Cook's Voyages

NORTH AMERICA
OCEANIA
SOUTH AMERICA

1768–71
1772–75
1776–79

Who found new plants and animals?

Botanist **Joseph Banks** travelled on Captain Cook's ship *Endeavour*. Banks took advantage of the lands they visited, studying, drawing and collecting thousands of species.

> On our travels, I saw a strange animal that the locals called a 'gangurru'.

> And I saw a strange dude drawing me!

Who got sent to cross America?

President Jefferson sent **Meriwether Lewis** and **William Clark** to explore the newly enlarged United States in 1803. Much of the vast land was unmapped and the two explorers faced many dangers along the way.

We met lots of wild animals and were chased by grizzly bears!

Grrrr!

I stopped Lewis and Clark getting lost, found them food to eat, and helped them avoid conflict with local Native Americans.

Who saved the day?

A young Shoshone woman called **Sacagawea** acted as a translator and guide for Lewis and Clark. She took her newborn baby boy with her, travelling thousands of kilometres to the Pacific Ocean and back.

How did camels get to Australia?

When Europeans started exploring inland Australia about 200 years ago, they brought camels from India that were used to trekking in very dry conditions.

Aboriginal peoples had been living in Australia for more than 70,000 years before Europeans arrived.

There are now more than one million wild camels in Australia!

Why was crossing Australia so hard?

Scorching temperatures and scarce water made finding a route across the country very tough. A prize of £2000 led different expeditions to attempt it in the 1860s, but some would die trying.

We made it from the south to the north coast in 1861...

I made it to the north coast and back in 1862 on my third attempt, and claimed the prize money.

...but died on the way home.

William Wills

Robert Burke

John McDouall Stuart

Who went on African adventures?

Many European explorers travelled in Africa in the 1800s – a time when there weren't any maps for large parts of the continent. They all wanted to say they had got somewhere 'first'.

Europeans were enthralled by tales of new-to-them lands brought back by explorers. Of course, these places had been populated for many thousands of years by African people.

Who looked for the source of the Nile?

John Speke and **Richard Burton** trekked many miles looking for the start of the river Nile, which they thought flowed from a lake in the middle of Africa.

Speke named the lake Victoria, after Queen Victoria.

They caught many tropical diseases and were often sick.

Richard got sick and had to stop and rest. John kept going, eventually finding the lake in 1858, becoming the first European to see it.

Where was Livingstone lost?

Famous Victorian explorer **Dr David Livingstone** went missing in East Africa in the 1860s. He had walked right across Africa, sailed down the Zambezi and was the first European to see the *Mosi-oa-Tunya* waterfall, which he named Victoria Falls.

Livingstone was mauled by a lion on his travels.

Who found him?

Writer and explorer **Henry Stanley** went to look for Livingstone, eventually finding him in Tanzania in 1871.

Who took grand expeditions to the Nile?

Women had few chances to become explorers in the 1800s but a young Dutch woman, **Alexine Tinné**, threw herself into travel. Along with her mother, she visited the vast area around the Nile river in the 1860s.

In 1869, Alexine tried to cross the huge Sahara Desert but was sadly killed in a raid.

David Livingstone said Tinné was the best explorer he knew!

Would you rather?

Go exploring in a **plane**...

...or onboard a **sailing boat**?

Explore a **baking hot** desert...

Phew!

Visit unexplored parts of **Earth**...

...or unexplored parts of the **Moon**?

Discover a new **plant**...

Who got to the North Pole first?

Believe it or not, people have been arguing about this for years! Because the North Pole is in the frozen Arctic ice, it was very hard for explorers to tell if they'd got there or not!

Roald Amundsen (Norwegian)

"The actual winner was me! I flew over the top of the pole in May 1926 in an airship."

"We thought we'd got there in April 1909 but experts think we hadn't quite made it."

Robert Peary and Matthew Henson (American)

Frederick Cook (American)

"I said I'd got there on foot in April 1908, but couldn't prove it."

"I was the first Black American Arctic explorer and had to fight for my achievements to be recognized."

How did Jo Peary help?

Jo Peary went on many adventures with her husband Robert at a time when women usually stayed at home. An explorer in her own right, she organized a rescue mission when Robert was stranded on the wrong side of an ice cap!

i gave birth to my daughter, Marie, while travelling in the Arctic!

i was the first person who definitely got there on foot, and that wasn't until 1969!

Wally Herbert (British)

You just missed them.

We've blown it, chaps!

You don't say!

Who raced to the South Pole?

A Norwegian team, led by **Roald Amundsen**, and a British expedition, led by **Robert Falcon Scott**. Amundsen reached the pole in December 1911 and Scott's team arrived a month later, but died on the return journey.

Who stood on top of the world?

On 29 May 1953, New Zealander **Edmund Hillary** and Nepalese mountaineer **Tenzing Norgay** became the first people to climb the 8849-metre high Mount Everest in the Himalayas. The world's highest mountain had been conquered at last.

I saved Edmund's life when we were practising for the climb and he fell into a crevasse.

Who climbed Everest — and more?

On 16 May 1975, Japanese mountaineer **Junko Tabei** became the first woman to conquer Everest. In 1992, she then became the first woman to climb the Seven Summits, the highest mountain on each continent. Her motto was...

Do not give up. Keep on your quest.

Tenzing Norgay

Edmund Hillary

We've made it to the top of the world!

Who was the first man in space?

Russian cosmonaut **Yuri Gagarin** blasted off into space on 12 April 1961 in the *Vostok 1* capsule. He whizzed once around the planet before landing back on Earth one hour and 48 minutes later.

Have you come from outer space?

As a matter of fact, I have.

Gagarin landed in a potato field, scaring the local villagers.

And who was the first woman?

Valentina Tereshkova became the first woman in space when she orbited Earth, alone, for just under three days in June 1963. She was only 26 years old at the time.

I'm still the only woman to have been on a solo space mission and the youngest to have been to space.

How long did it take to fly to the Moon?

It took 4 days, 6 hours, 45 minutes and 40 seconds for the first people to get to the Moon. After landing, **Neil Armstrong** became the first human to walk on its surface, on 21 July 1969, followed by **Buzz Aldrin**.

Neil, Buzz and Michael were on NASA's Apollo 11 mission.

I'm Michael Collins and I stayed flying in the command module that took us all back to Earth.

Command module

Service module

Hey, Neil, take my picture!

Our moonwalk lasted for around 2 hours.

Buzz Aldrin

Lunar module 'Eagle'

Neil Armstrong

A compendium of questions

Who never gave up?

Ernest Shackleton was exploring Antarctica in 1914 when his ship got crushed by ice. The crew eventually sailed to a tiny island in lifeboats, then a small group braved terrible seas to get to another island for help.

It took nearly 18 months from getting stuck to rescuing everyone!

Who left his heart behind?

When explorer **David Livingstone** died in 1873, his heart was buried in Africa, while the rest of his body was returned to England.

Who circled the globe?

Epic adventurer **Ranulph Fiennes** travelled from north to south around the poles between 1979 and 1982, without using planes.

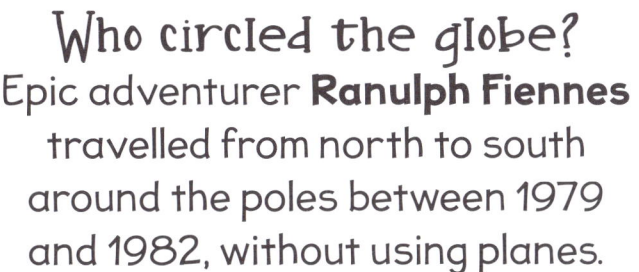

i'm Bothie — I went on the expeditions too, and became the first dog to visit both Poles.

i became one of the world's most popular travel writers.

Where is the Valley of the Assassins?

This legendary place with a ruined medieval fortress is in northern Iran. British-Italian explorer, **Freya Stark**, was the first Westerner to trek to it in 1931.

Who broke boundaries?

In 1992, doctor and astronaut **Mae Jemison** orbited Earth on the space shuttle *Endeavour*, becoming the first woman of colour to travel in space.

There are still many mountains to climb, rivers to navigate, and jungles to map.

I'm actually afraid of heights!

Is there anywhere left to explore?

Yes! Only 20 percent of the world's oceans have been fully explored, and just 5 percent of the seabed.

Who missed Australia?

"We're over here!"

In 1642, Dutch explorer **Abel Tasman** landed in Van Diemen's Land (now called Tasmania) and reached New Zealand, but sailed right around Australia without noticing it!

"Sorry we're late!"

"It took us nine months to get here!"

Will we ever walk on Mars?

Mars has been visited by spacecraft, but it has no breathable air and its surface temperature is below freezing. Despite this, many space agencies are working on plans to send humans to Mars.

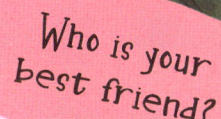

INCREDIBLE JOURNEYS

Why go on a journey?

Since humans first existed, we've explored and travelled. We go on journeys to see new places and things, meet new people and have amazing adventures!

I set off in 1884 and completed my journey in 1886. I cycled about 22,000 kilometres!

Stevens's route

Who did it first?

People sometimes try to be the first to do a particular journey, whether that's to the top of a mountain or across an ocean. **Thomas Stevens** was first to cycle around the world.

He crossed the oceans by boat, obviously!

Penny farthing bicycle

Mum's drive was the first long-distance car journey.

Steering wheel

The Benz Patent-Motorwagen

How would you like to travel?

Whenever new forms of transport are invented, people try to make incredible journeys using them. **Bertha Benz** drove 194 kilometres in 1888 to whip up interest in the motorcar, which had recently been invented by her husband, Karl Benz.

What could possibly go wrong?

Lots of things — and they often remain a mystery. Japanese adventurer **Naomi Uemura** was the first person to reach the North Pole alone and to raft the Amazon solo. But he set off to climb the Alaskan mountain Denali in 1984, and never returned.

I had already climbed Denali solo. My second try was in winter, so conditions were more dangerous.

Can you go around the world in 80 days?

In Jules Verne's 1872 novel, Phileas Fogg travels around the world in 80 days. In a time before cars or planes, this seemed an impossible feat. But someone soon attempted it for real!

Could Nellie make it?

In 1889, American news writer **Nellie Bly** set off to see if she really could go around the world in under 80 days. She did it in 72, setting a new world record!

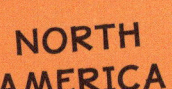

Bly's route

Concorde's route

NORTH AMERICA

ATLANTIC OCEAN

SOUTH AMERICA

PACIFIC OCEAN

Magellan's route

Nellie travelled by steamship, train, horse-drawn carriage, tram, rickshaw, and donkey – that's me!

Who did it first?

The first ever around-the-world trip was led by Portuguese explorer **Ferdinand Magellan**. The epic voyage began in 1519 and took 1084 days. Sadly, Magellan died on the way. Of a crew of 240, only 30 made it all the way home.

Who did it fastest?

In 1995, a supersonic Concorde jet made the fastest ever flight around the world. It took just under 32 hours.

Concorde

EUROPE

ASIA

PACIFIC OCEAN

Magellan set sail from Spain in 1519

AFRICA

INDIAN OCEAN

OCEANIA

Magellan died here in 1521

ATLANTIC OCEAN

International Space Station

If you count space travel, the record is much faster. I zoom around Earth in just 90 minutes!

47

Can you swim down the Amazon?

Slovenian swimmer **Martin Strel** swam the entire length of South America's Amazon River in 2007. He had to dodge deadly bull sharks and piranhas on the way.

The length of my Amazon swim was 5268 kilometres!

I was a soldier too – I lost my right arm in an American Civil War battle.

Where does this canyon go? In 1869, American explorer and geologist **John Wesley Powell** led the first expedition by boat down the Colorado River through the remote Grand Canyon in Arizona, USA. The journey made the canyon famous.

Who fought off a crocodile?

English explorer **Mary Kingsley** was famous for her journeys in Africa. In 1895, a crocodile climbed onto her canoe as she paddled up the Ogooué River in Gabon.

Biff!

I had to fend the croc off with my paddle. I was terrified, but I survived!

Strap

Cushion

Lead weights

Who went over the falls in a barrel?

In 1901, 63-year-old retired teacher **Annie Edson Taylor** became the first person to go down 51-metre-high Niagara Falls in a barrel (and survive!). The trip was NOT fun. Afterwards, Annie said, "No one ought ever to do that again!"

Annie designed the barrel herself!

Did you know?

In 1993, Japanese yachtsman Kenichi Horie made the longest journey by pedal-powered boat — **7500 kilometres** from Hawaii to Japan.

We explored 2212 metres!

The **deepest trip underground** was made by Pavel Demidov and his team in 2018, at the Verevnika Cave in Georgia.

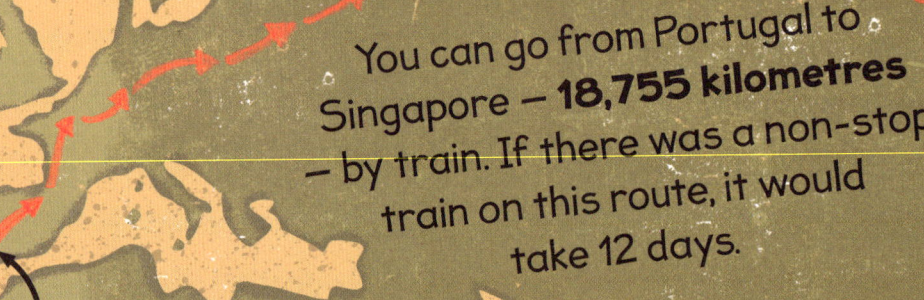

You can go from Portugal to Singapore — **18,755 kilometres** — by train. If there was a non-stop train on this route, it would take 12 days.

Portugal

Singapore

Only one more week of climbing to go!

The first time climbers made it up Canada's Mount Thor, the world's **tallest vertical cliff face**, it took them 33 days!

Are we nearly there?

In 1964, Reg Spiers made the journey from the UK to Australia by **posting** himself inside a large box!

Ashley Battles broke the record for the **longest-lasting wing walk** in 2010, by flying along on top of a plane's wing for 4 hours and 2 minutes.

It feels like I'm on top of the world!

I free-floated 98 metres away from the Space Shuttle.

In 1984, US astronaut Bruce McCandless became the first person to go on an **untethered spacewalk**.

Vikings often took their boats out of the water and **carried or dragged** them over land to get to a new river or sea.

In 2013, British adventurer Sarah Outen **rowed** across the Pacific, taking 150 days to get from Japan to Alaska.

An Astute-class submarine can patrol underwater for **25 years** before it needs to come to the surface to refuel.

Who crossed the Pacific first?

Ferdinand Magellan and his crew were first to sail across the Pacific, on their around-the-world trip in 1521... or WERE they? Norwegian explorer **Thor Heyerdahl** wasn't so sure.

Wood and bamboo masts

Kon-Tiki

Lightweight balsa wood logs

What did Thor think?

Heyerdahl believed ancient people could have sailed across the Pacific on simple rafts, long before Magellan's voyage. A trail of clues indicate that Pacific Islanders and native Americans may have met up thousands of years ago.

Deep-sea canoe, used by ancient Polynesians

① Similar canoes in North America and Polynesia, made by sewing planks together.

Who escaped from Antarctica?

In 1914, Irish adventurer **Ernest Shackleton** set off with a crew of men in his ship *Endurance*, to trek across Antarctica. But they soon faced a life-or-death struggle to survive.

Ernest Shackleton

① What went wrong?

As *Endurance* sailed towards Antarctica, it got trapped in sea ice.

② How did the ship sink?

The floating ice dragged *Endurance* off course. It was trapped for ten months, before being crushed by the pressure of the ice.

Luckily the crew rescued lifeboats and supplies before it sank!

③ Who went to get help?

The men camped on the ice until it melted enough for them to sail to nearby Elephant Island. Then Shackleton and five others set off in a lifeboat to raise the alarm.

The rest of the crew were left behind.

④

We didn't know when – or if – Shackleton would come back.

How did the crew survive?

They used the two remaining lifeboats, upturned, as shelter, and shared out their dwindling supplies as slowly as they could.

⑤ Did everyone get home?

Seventeen days and 1300 kilometres later Shackleton reached South Georgia. He returned on a bigger boat for the stranded team.

Every last man was rescued!

⑥ What happened to the *Endurance*?

The wreck of *Endurance* was finally discovered on the seabed in 2022!

How many?

19 The age of **Zara Rutherford** when she flew solo around the world, from 2021–2022.

Tiny Cessna 172

A truck on the ground refuelled the plane twice a day.

The longest continuous plane flight lasted for **64** days, from December 1958 to February 1959.

Canadian explorer **Aloha Wanderwell** spent **5** years going around the world in a Ford Model T, an early model of car.

The world's shortest airline flight, between the islands of Westray and Papa Westray in Scotland, UK, takes just **1** minute.

Some freight trains in Canada can be **4.2** kilometres long!

How high can you jump from?

A balloon filled with helium gas instead of hot air can go super high. In 2014, engineer **Alan Eustace** soared to 41,419 metres – then returned to the ground by parachute!

How high can you fly?

In 2005, Indian aviator **Vijaypat Singhania** flew into the record books by making the highest-ever hot-air balloon journey – 21,290 metres.

Can a balloon fly around the world?

Yes! **Bertrand Piccard** and **Brian Jones** did it in 2000 in their huge high-altitude balloon, Breitling Orbiter 3 – taking almost 20 days.

Who was the first female balloonist?

French balloonist **Sophie Blanchard** was the first woman to fly solo in a balloon, in 1809. As well as flying across the Alps, she performed balloon displays, doing tricks and launching fireworks.

Flight is an incomparable sensation!

Blanchard's balloon basket was tiny

I went so high, I had to wear a spacesuit!

Who flew so high he passed out?

In 1862, **James Glaisher** fainted from lack of oxygen when he and **Henry Coxwell** flew to 8800 metres – higher than anyone had before. Coxwell's fingers froze, so he had to pull on a cord with his teeth to bring the balloon down safely.

59

Why did Darwin travel the world?

In 1831, a ship named the *Beagle* set off from England on a five-year journey. **Charles Darwin**, a young naturalist, was on board to study rocks and wildlife.

① Darwin studied different species of finches in the Galápagos Islands.

② Darwin noticed that the finches in different locations had small differences.

What did Darwin discover?

Along the way, Darwin found many amazing species and fossils. They helped him understand evolution – the way living things change over time.

Living things change and branch off from each other, like the branches of a tree!

③ Darwin realized that the finches had adapted (changed over time) in ways that helped them survive in their different environments.

How far did Humboldt go?

From 1799 to 1804, German naturalist and explorer **Alexander von Humboldt** journeyed over 9600 kilometres through parts of north, south and central America and the Caribbean.

I travelled by canoe, on foot and on horseback.

Alexander von Humboldt

Mexico

CENTRAL AMERICA

Humboldt's journey

How can an eel frighten a horse?

Humboldt wanted to study electric eels, so the local people said they would catch some for him. They led their horses into the river, and the eels jumped out of the water and gave them electric shocks!

Do you fancy a swim?

Hmmm... I don't think so!

Who went in search of new caterpillars?

In 1699, Swiss scientist and artist **Maria Sibylla Merian** sailed all the way to Suriname to study its caterpillars. Until Merian recorded the process of metamorphosis, many people thought that butterflies came from mud!

Merian explored Suriname from 1699 to 1701.

Who walked through a flooded forest?

English adventurer **Ed Stafford** and his Peruvian guide **Gadiel Sanchez Rivera** WALKED across the Amazon rainforest, following the Amazon River. The journey of more than 6000 kilometres took 860 days.

We slept in comfortable hammock systems with big mosquito nets.

Who vanished into thin air?

After setting several flight records, famous aviator **Amelia Earhart** began a round-the-world journey in 1937. She was almost home when her plane vanished near Howland Island (her next stop) in the Pacific Ocean.

There's more to life than being a passenger! I love being the pilot!

Earhart was never seen again. Some say she could have survived if she crash-landed on Nikumaroro Island.

Who nearly flew into a huge waterfall?

American pilot **Jimmie Angel** did! He was flying over the Venezuelan jungle in 1933 when he almost hit the world's tallest waterfall. Called *Kerepakupai Meru* by the local Pemon people, the falls became known to outsiders as Angel Falls.

The falls' indigenous name means 'Water of the deepest place'. They are 979 metres high!

Who hovered his way across the sea?

In 2019, French inventor **Franky Zapata** became the first person ever to cross the English Channel on a hoverboard.

Can you pedal a plane?

Yes! **Bryan Allen** flew across the English Channel in 1979. That alone wouldn't be remarkable, but Allen was a cyclist, and the plane, the *Gossamer Albatross*, was pedal-powered. Phew!

The Gossamer Albatross's top speed was only 29 kilometres an hour!

67

What went wrong on Apollo 13?

In 1970, three astronauts set off in the *Apollo 13* spacecraft. They were meant to land on the Moon, but on the way, an oxygen tank exploded and the cabin lost oxygen and power.

① On 11 April the rocket carrying the Apollo 13 spacecraft took off from the Kennedy Space Center in Florida, USA.

② Two days into the journey, astronaut Jack Swigert switched on a fan to stir the oxygen tanks — something they did every day. There was a bang and the oxygen escaped into space!

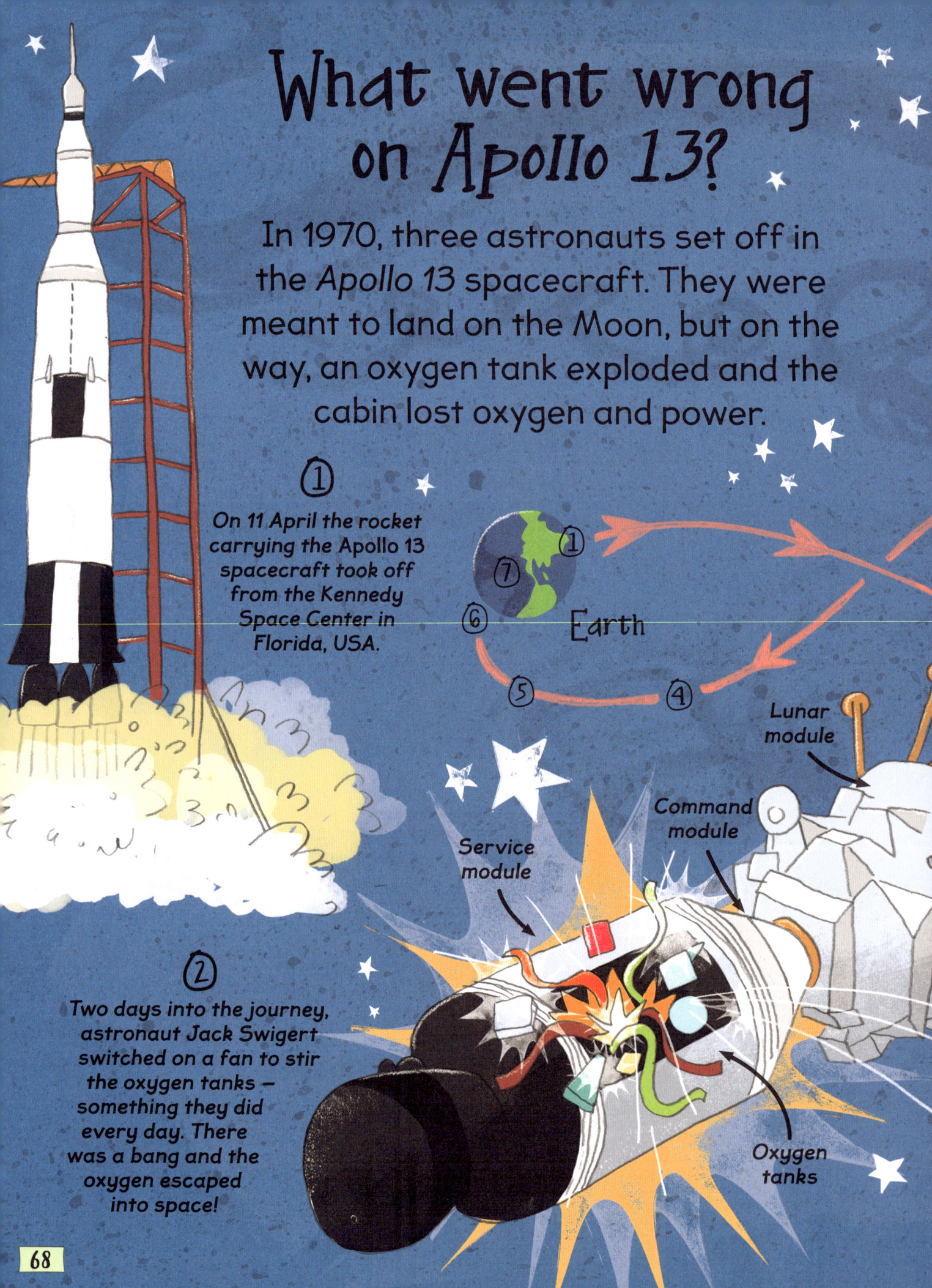

③ **Did they make it to the Moon?**
No – the crew had to abandon their main craft and escape into the tiny lunar module, designed for landing on the Moon's surface. Then, they looped around the Moon and headed home.

④ The lunar module had enough oxygen, but the crew had to build makeshift equipment to clean the air they were breathing out.

⑤ On day six, as the crew approached Earth, they jettisoned the damaged service module.

⑥ The crew climbed back into the cone-shaped command module, and separated it from the lunar module to return to Earth.

⑦ **Did they get home?**
Yes – the command module splashed down safely into the Pacific Ocean, and the crew were rescued.

A compendium of questions

How long can a plane fly upside down?

American stunt pilot Joann Osterud flew her biplane upside-down for 4 hours and 38 minutes in 1991, covering a distance of 1059 kilometres.

How far can you go underground?

The Gotthard Base Tunnel in Switzerland burrows under the Alps, stretching 57 kilometres between the towns of Erstfeld and Bodio.

What do you do if you see a mermaid?

If you're **Henry Hudson**, you record the sighting in your ship's log book! He wrote that the mermaid had pale skin, dark hair and a porpoise-like tail.

We'll never know what Hudson really saw!

Who's been to space AND the bottom of the sea?

After a career as a NASA astronaut, **Kathy Sullivan** went on a dive to the bottom of Challenger Deep, the deepest part of the sea, in 2020.

Have you ever seen a submersible like this before?

Who got lost looking for a lost city?

In 1925, English adventurer **Percy Fawcett** went into the Amazon jungle to search for an ancient city, which he named the City of Z. He was never seen again...

How far do we all travel every day?

About 47 million kilometres — as that's how fast the Earth is flying through space!

If I slow down, everyone's birthdays will be late!

Why was Pytheas puzzled?

Ancient Greek explorer **Pytheas** travelled north from Massalia (in today's France), perhaps as far as Iceland. He described how, in midsummer, the Sun didn't go down for several days!

It was more than four years until I was rescued!

Who was the REAL Robinson Crusoe?

Daniel Defoe's 1719 book, which tells the tale of a castaway on a desert island, was based on a real person! **Alexander Selkirk** was a Scottish sailor who was marooned on an island in the Pacific.

Can you work a robot?

What's your favourite food?

What's your favourite colour?

Which invention in this book do you think is the best?

CLEVER INVENTORS

Are all inventions new?

Some are, but usually inventors look at something that already exists then change it, to make it even better.

"This is hard work! What if I add some pedals?"

1817 – Laufmaschine 'running machine' by Karl Drais.

"This is a bumpy ride! What if I make the front wheel bigger?"

1861 – Michaudine 'boneshaker' by Pierre and Ernest Michaux.

Do inventions ever get stolen?

"Yes, someone stole my idea for making flat-bottomed paper bags. I had to take them to court – and I won!"

Margaret Knight invented lots of things, including a safety device for a factory machine in 1850, when she was just 12 years old.

What is an inventor?

Anyone who designs or builds something new is called an inventor. Some people have many ideas; others have just one brilliant idea.

In the 1870s, James Bedford Elliott took the big wheel off the penny farthing to create a unicycle.

It's dangerous being so high up. What if the seat was lower and I added a chain?

1871 – Ariel 'penny farthing' by James Starley.

1885 – Rover 'safety bicycle' by John Starley.

Modern bikes have almost the same design as the Rover!

Which invention lit up the world?

After the discovery of fire, ancient humans invented little oil-burning lamps to see in the dark. They also made tools, mirrors and wheels.

Hand axes chipped from flint were used almost two million years ago.

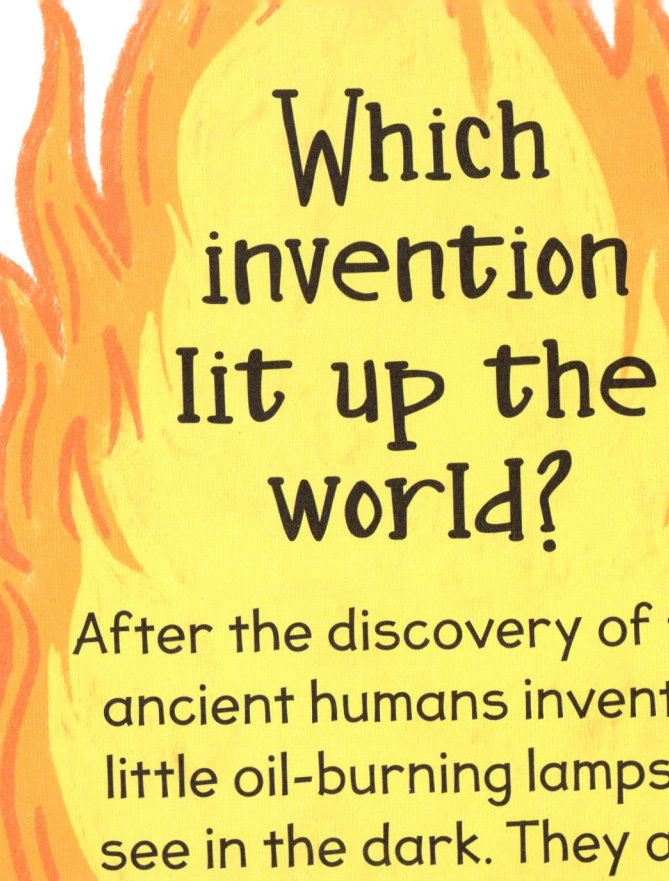

Oil lamp

The earliest mirrors were made 8000 years ago out of polished black glassy rock.

People living long ago also invented wheels, and shaped clay into pots. Later they made carts.

Who started scribbling?

People came up with different ways of writing all around the world.

The ancient Sumerians (4500–1900 BCE) invented a way of writing, called cuneiform.

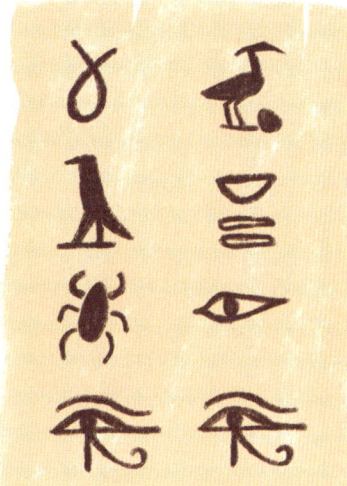

The ancient Egyptians (around 3100 BCE) wrote in little pictures, called hieroglyphs.

The Ancient Chinese (around 1250 BCE) wrote in characters called Hanzi.

好奇

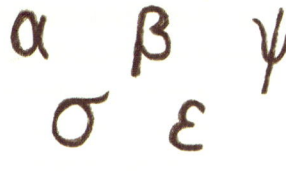

The Phoenicians, ancient Greeks and ancient Romans (between 1500 BCE and 750 BCE) wrote in an alphabet, which records the sound of speech.

How did millions of people end up with books?

Johannes Gutenberg's book printing press of the 1400s made books easier to make and cheaper to buy. Before the print press, books had to be copied out by hand, which took ages!

Today we can use an e-reader to read books. The first ones were created in the 1990s.

A screw presses paper onto moveable metal letters.

The letters are covered with ink and make an exact copy each time.

79

Did you know?

In the 1800s **Josephine Cochran** invented the dishwasher. Big dishwashers were first used by hotels and restaurants.

Emojis were created in 1999 by **Shigetaka Kurita**. The first emojis all had just 144 pixels (little squares of data).

Smaller dishwashers didn't make it into people's homes until the 1950s.

A new fizzy drink was made by **Dr John Pemberton** in his yard in 1886. He sold it as a 'brain tonic' and it became the world-famous Coca Cola.

Alan Turing was an amazing mathematician who worked for the British government during World War II as a code-breaker.

Alan Turing's bomb code-breaking machine

American president **Theodore Roosevelt Jr** was also known as Teddy. He hadn't wanted to shoot a real bear on a hunting trip and a toymaker made a stuffed bear of him and named it 'Teddy's bear'.

Denim jeans were created by **Jacob W Davis** and **Levi Strauss** in the 1870s for goldminers, who needed hard-wearing clothes.

The 24-hour clock for the whole world was devised by **Sandford Fleming** in 1876, later called 'Cosmic Time'.

Play-Doh, invented by the **McVicker** family in the 1930s, started out as something to clean soot off wallpaper!

John Logie Baird's first attempt at creating a television in 1923 was made using a hat box, knitting needles and bicycle lamps!

Who was ahead of his time?

Leonardo da Vinci was one of the world's cleverest inventors. He lived over 500 years ago, but he came up with futuristic ideas for all kinds of things long before people knew how to build them.

A winged flying machine.

I was interested in space, flight, how bodies work, science, painting, mathematics and sculpture.

A battle tank covered with metal plates, which had a turret on top to fire weapons through.

A machine with a turning spiral at the top and blades to power it into the air.

How did da Vinci record his ideas?

Put a mirror here

Leonardo used mirror writing in his notebooks – maybe so other people didn't steal his clever ideas!

Who else had awesome, ancient ideas?

Archimedes (287–212 BCE) invented a huge wooden screw to raise water from rivers.

Chinese inventor **Zhang Heng** devised a way to detect distant earthquakes in 132 AD.

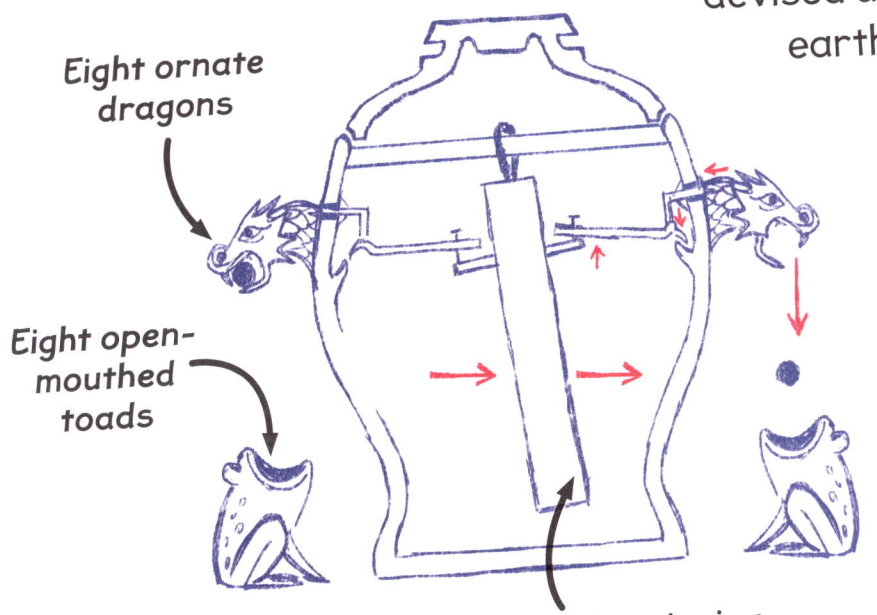

Eight ornate dragons

Eight open-mouthed toads

Bronze urn with swinging pendulum inside

The dragons, each with a copper ball, faced different directions. When a tremor was felt, the pendulum swung and a ball from the direction of the tremor dropped down to the toad.

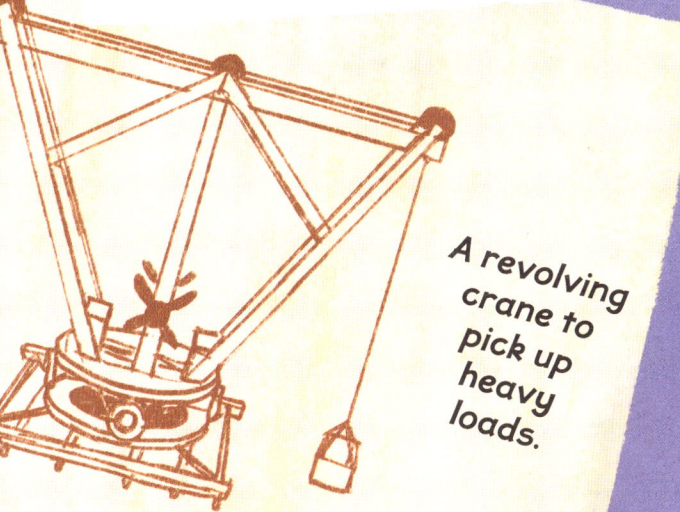

A revolving crane to pick up heavy loads.

Engineer **Ismail Al-Jazari** (1136–1206) invented intricate clocks, locks and all sorts of mechanical toys.

Who got us moving?

Early transport inventions were often created by people working alone. Nowadays, entire teams of people work together to develop ideas.

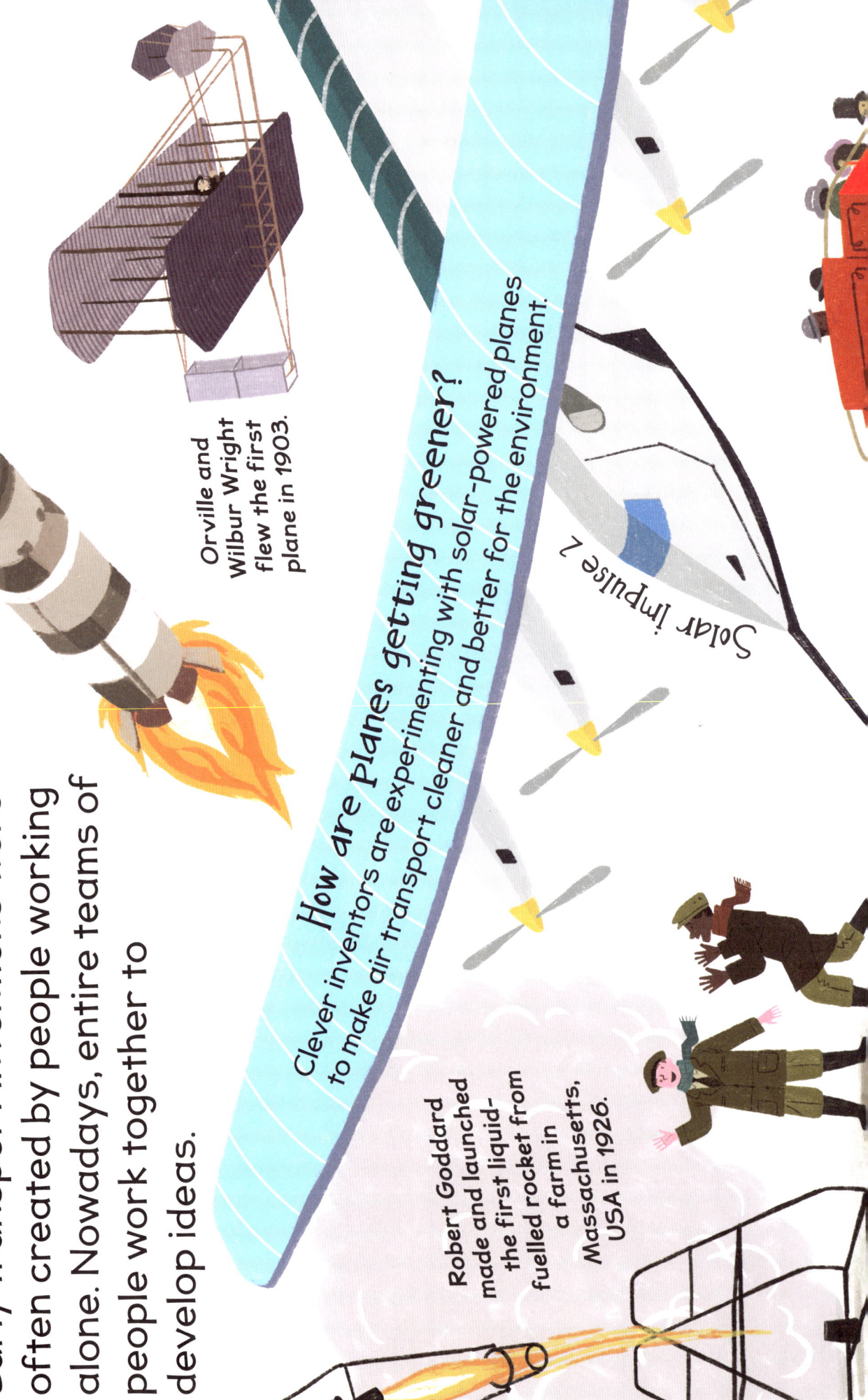

Wernher von Braun and his team at NASA designed the Saturn V rockets in the 1960s, which took astronauts to the Moon.

Orville and Wilbur Wright flew the first plane in 1903.

How are planes getting greener?

Clever inventors are experimenting with solar-powered planes to make air transport cleaner and better for the environment.

Solar Impulse 2

Robert Goddard made and launched the first liquid-fuelled rocket from a farm in Massachusetts, USA in 1926.

I did! I'm Frank Searle. In 1909, I designed the first London double-decker bus.

The PlanetSolar built by the Knierim shipyard, was the first solar-powered boat to sail around the world between 2010 and 2012.

Who had a wheelie good idea?

I did, in 1885 I'm Karl Benz. My car had three wheels and could only travel at 16 kilometres an hour!

How did we learn to float a boat?

Early people worked out how to carve simple boats from tree trunks. Later, people built boats with sails that could be pushed by the wind.

How many?

5127 prototypes made by inventor **James Dyson** before he got his new bagless vacuum cleaner just right.

748,626 US patent number of 'The Landlord's Game', also known as 'Monopoly', invented by **Lizzie J Magie** in 1904.

Fugaku, one of the world's fastest supercomputers can work at **442 quadrillion** (one thousand trillion) calculations a second.

Famous US inventor, **Thomas Edison**, said, "Genius is **1** percent inspiration, **99** percent perspiration."

Today, there are over 100 colours of crayon with names like Robin's Egg Blue and Jazzberry Jam.

colours in the first-ever box of Crayola crayons, invented by **Edwin Binney** and **C. Harold Smith** in 1903.

320 kilometres an hour. Top speed of Japanese Shinkansen 'bullet trains' designed by **Hideo Shima** and his team of engineers in 1964.

48 kilometres an hour.

Top speed of the Rocket, one of the world's first-ever steam locomotives, invented by **George Stephenson** in 1829.

355 inventions patented by **Alfred Nobel**, including one for dynamite. He requested the Nobel Prize be set up in his name in 1896.

Bill Gates, chairman of Microsoft Corporation bought one of Leonardo da Vinci's surviving notebooks, in 1994 for...

US$30 million

Gymnast **George Nissen** was **16** when he invented the trampoline in the 1930s.

Who was a bright spark?

American inventor **Benjamin Franklin** flew a kite into a storm in 1752 to see whether electrical energy could be conducted. Many inventors then experimented with electricity as a usable power source.

Alessandro Volta (1745–1827) created the first electric battery.

My kite had a metal key attached to it and a wet string to conduct the 'electric fire' of the lightning.

Don't try this at home!

Humphry Davy (1778–1829) worked out how an electrical current could create light.

Michael Faraday (1791–1867) made the first electro-magnetic generator turning movement into power.

Which inventions have saved lives?

When a pandemic (a worldwide disease) was declared in March 2020, the Covid-19 vaccine was created, developed and tested in a matter of months. It has saved millions of lives.

The first microscope was created in the 1600s to better understand disease. Microbiology is the study of microscopic organisms.

As technology improved, scientists could begin to see how tiny organisms like viruses and bacteria could cause illnesses and disease.

Who has helped athletes run like cheetahs?

Van Phillips, who lost one of his legs, is the inventor of Flex-Foot prosthetic limbs. The Flex-Foot Cheetah has a carbon-fibre blade to help athletes run fast.

What helps to see inside our bodies?

X-rays are used to look inside us to check for lumps, bumps and broken bones. **Wilhelm Röntgen** took the first-ever X-ray in 1895. It was of his wife's hand.

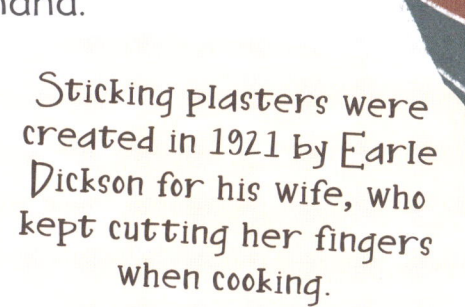

Sticking plasters were created in 1921 by Earle Dickson for his wife, who kept cutting her fingers when cooking.

Plaster cast

Blade flexes on impact with the ground

When was the first plaster cast?

Long ago, people used wooden splints and other methods to set broken bones. During World War I, **Anne Acheson** developed a way of using plaster of Paris to help set broken bones in a cast. This kind of plaster cast is still used today.

91

Would you rather?

Meet **Leonardo da Vinci** or...

...**Markus Persson**, the creator of Minecraft?

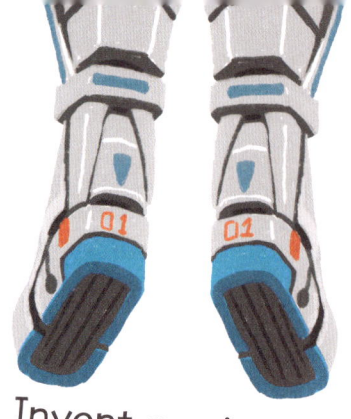

Invent a pair of winged hover **boots** or a **plane** with flapping wings?

Take a trip on the **fastest train** in the world or...

...ride an early '**penny farthing**'?

Create a new kind of chocolate bar like Francis Fry or a new kind of breakfast cereal like Joseph Kellogg?

The Fry family sold drinking chocolate, but **Francis Fry** was the first person to make chocolate into a solid bar in 1847.

Who was the 'father of the computer'?

In the 1830s, **Charles Babbage** designed two clever computing machines to store and process numbers. His friend, **Ada Lovelace**, wrote the first computing code to one of his machines.

I didn't get round to completing my computing machines but if I had, one of them might have looked a bit like this...

Babbage's proposed Analytical Engine is considered to be the first ever computer

Charles Babbage

In the 1940s an enormous electric computer called ENIAC was built. Today, the whole processing power and speed of ENIAC can be fitted on to one tiny silicon chip!

When were supercomputers invented?

Seymour Cray built the first superfast supercomputer in 1976. It was giant, and it got so hot it had to have a special cooling system to stop it melting.

Who was the 'mother of Wifi'?

Hedy Lamarr was a famous Hollywood actress, but her real love was inventing. During World War II she invented a type of frequency hopping technology.

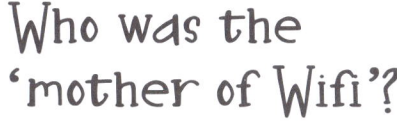

My invention became the basis for today's Wifi and Bluetooth!

How do computers talk to each other?

Tim Berners-Lee created a universal computing language known as hypertext markup language (HTML) in 1989. It was the beginning of the World Wide Web and he gave his invention to the world for free, without taking out any patents.

Are things ever invented by accident?

Once set in motion the Slinky transfers energy along its length to allow it to 'walk'.

Yes! When naval engineer **Richard James** dropped a spring he was working with in 1943, he was stunned to see it 'walk' down a stack of books onto the floor. Soon, he'd invented Slinky toys!

Frank Epperson

When I was 11, I created the first ice lolly. I left my drink outside overnight with a stirring stick in it. In the morning it had frozen!

Who had a blast with water?

Space engineer **Lonnie Johnson** did! He came up with the idea for a Super Soaker water gun in 1989 when he accidentally fired water across his bathroom while doing an experiment for a new space mission.

Whose sticky glue idea came unstuck?

In 1968, **Spencer Silver** was trying to invent a new, extra-strong glue, but it just wasn't sticky, so he gave up...

...A few years later, **Arthur Fry** used Silver's accidental invention of non-sticky glue to make reusable bookmarks or 'post-it' notes.

Which tasty cereal was made by mistake?

The Kellogg brothers tried to make granola in 1898, but accidentally flaked wheat berries instead.

Then they tried flaking corn and invented a whole new breakfast cereal!

Lonnie Johnson

Whose inventions are helping our planet?

As Earth is so polluted by plastic litter and dirty gases, clever inventors are now busy trying to create clean energy and tidy up the mess we've made.

What kind of snake is cleaning our oceans?

A long, snake-like floating barrier was invented by **Boyan Slat** in 2017. Called the Ocean Cleanup system, the 'snake' gathers up plastic and other pollution floating in our oceans, so it can be recycled.

A 3-metre skirt beneath the surface lets marine life pass through

The Ocean Cleanup system is busy tackling the Great Pacific Garbage Patch — a mass of floating rubbish twice the size of France.

Support vessel

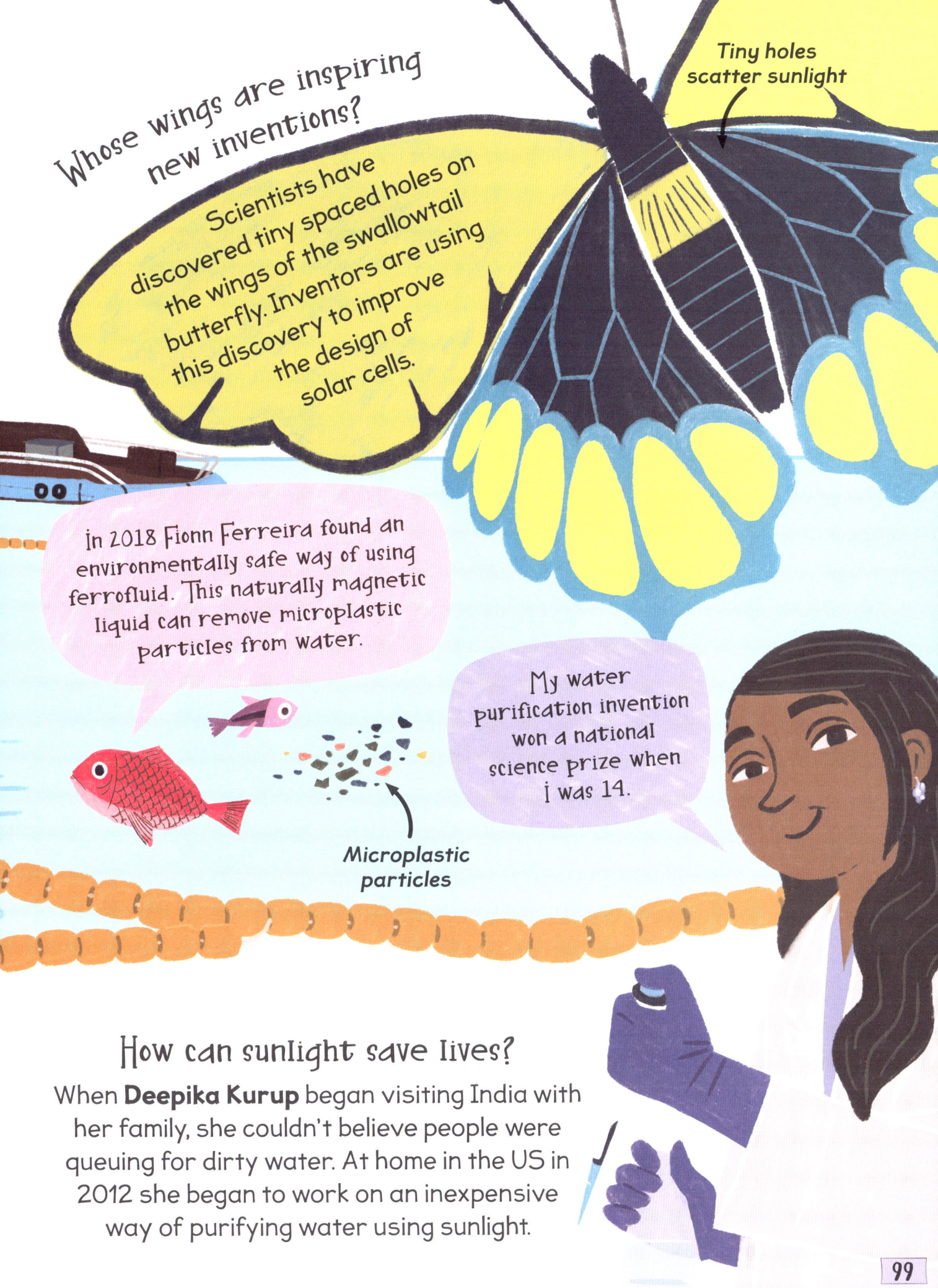

Whose wings are inspiring new inventions?

Scientists have discovered tiny spaced holes on the wings of the swallowtail butterfly. Inventors are using this discovery to improve the design of solar cells.

Tiny holes scatter sunlight

In 2018 Fionn Ferreira found an environmentally safe way of using ferrofluid. This naturally magnetic liquid can remove microplastic particles from water.

Microplastic particles

My water purification invention won a national science prize when I was 14.

How can sunlight save lives?

When **Deepika Kurup** began visiting India with her family, she couldn't believe people were queuing for dirty water. At home in the US in 2012 she began to work on an inexpensive way of purifying water using sunlight.

Can kids be inventors?

Yes! Some incredible things have been thought up by people not much older than you. You could invent a device to help people, a new kind of fuel, or a way to make a favourite toy even better.

Be inquisitive, determined and persistent like Richard. Use your imagination! Wonder 'what if' and always ask LOTS of curious questions!

Richard Turere

A Kenyan Maasai herder, Richard Turere, was only 11 years old when he invented Lion Lights. He connected a string of torches to an old car battery to scare lions away from his tribe's cattle. Lion Lights are widely used across Kenya today.

Ruth Amos

Ruth invented the StairSteady, to help people up and down stairs, as part of a school project when she was 15. She now has a YouTube channel called "Kids Invent Stuff" where you can send ideas for her to build on camera!

Ann Makosinski

A friend told Ann that she'd failed a test because her family didn't have electricity for her to study at night. So, in 2013, Ann invented a flashlight powered by the heat from its user's hand.

Shubham Banerjee

When he was 13 years old, Shubham invented a low-cost portable Braille printer, called the Braigo, using a Lego robotics kit.

Kylie Simonds

When ill with cancer in 2013, Kylie struggled to walk around with IV poles and wires. She invented an IV backpack for kids like her receiving chemotherapy or transfusions.

A compendium of questions

How did a plant inspire... ...some grippy stuff?

George de Mestral came up with the idea for Velcro in the 1950s, after examining the tiny burdock burrs caught in his dog's fur.

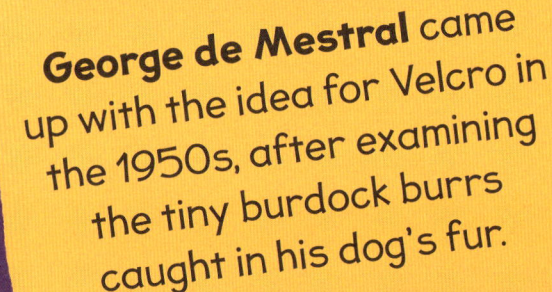

I was nicknamed 'Bluetooth' because of my blue/grey tooth!

Why is Bluetooth called Bluetooth?

Invented in 1994 by **Jaap Haartsen**, Bluetooth links electronic devices without cables. It's named after Harald Bluetooth, the 10th century King of Denmark, famous for uniting Scandinavia.

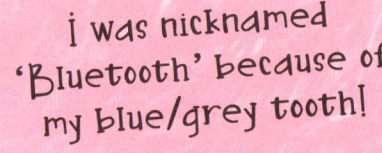

Who was nicknamed King Pong?

Nolan Bushnell was given the nickname after inventing Pong, one of the first video games in 1972 — two players had to bounce a ball over a net.

Why is my pen called a Biro?

Lots of companies now make ballpoint pens, but **László Bíró** was the inventor who came up with a way of making ink flow smoothly from a tiny ball instead of a nib.

What was created because of a love of fish?

The aquarium! **Jeanne Villepreux-Power** was so fascinated by marine life, she found a better way to study it by inventing the aquarium in 1832.

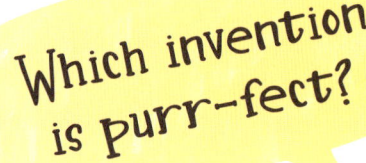

Which invention is purr-fect?

The cat's eye! In 1934, **Percy Shaw** created little cat's eye reflectors that could be placed along roads, after almost crashing his car in the dark.

Whose feet have inspired ideas?

Mine! I'm a gecko and my feet are covered in millions of tiny hairs, inspiring the invention of super-sticky bandages.

Who wanted kids to 'play well'?

Ole Kirk Christiansen's famous LEGO invention comes from two Danish words LEg GOdt, which mean 'play well'.

Lego was first made in 1958!

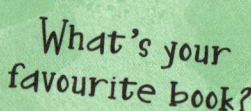

SUPER SCIENTISTS

How do scientists work?

Every scientist uses a special way of asking and answering questions called the **scientific method**.

What is a vaccine?

Vaccines are medicines that can protect us against diseases. In 2020, **Professor Sarah Gilbert** and her team made the first successful vaccine against COVID-19.

Who were the first scientists?

"Stargazing has its hazards!"

Long ago, people learnt how to do lots of clever things, like build pyramids, but they didn't know why things worked the way they did. To find the first scientists we have to go back thousands of years, to **ancient Greece**.

Eratosthenes measured the angles of shadows cast in two places on midsummer's day.

Who fell into a well?

Greek thinker **Thales** was interested in almost everything, including science, mathematics and engineering. Once, he was concentrating so much on the stars that he fell into a well!

Archimedes principle

An object floats in water if the force of its weight pushing down (gravity) is less than the weight of the water it pushes out of the way (buoyancy).

Who spilled the bathwater?

One day, **Archimedes** was sitting in his bath when he realized that the volume of water that was being pushed out was the same volume of his body that was under the water.

Maths can help us figure out all sorts of amazing things!

Who measured the Earth?

Eratosthenes was a mathematician and astronomer. He worked out a way of measuring the size of the Earth using the angle of shadows. His answer was very nearly right!

111

Who grasped gravity?

In the 1600s, **Isaac Newton** worked out that a force called gravity pulls things towards each other. So a tiny apple falls towards the big Earth.

Seeing an apple fall led me to the theory of gravity!

Newton worked out that gravity acts upon everything in the Universe.

Scientists do experiments to test their ideas.

Why doesn't the Moon fall from the sky?

The force of gravity holds the Moon in orbit around the Earth. The Moon travels fast enough to avoid crashing into the Earth but too slow to escape into space.

Pull of the Moon's gravity
Moon's speed
Moon
Pull of Earth's gravity
Earth

112

Who studies energy and matter?

Scientists who study the matter that everything is made of and the energy that makes things happen are called physicists. Physics is one of the oldest of the sciences.

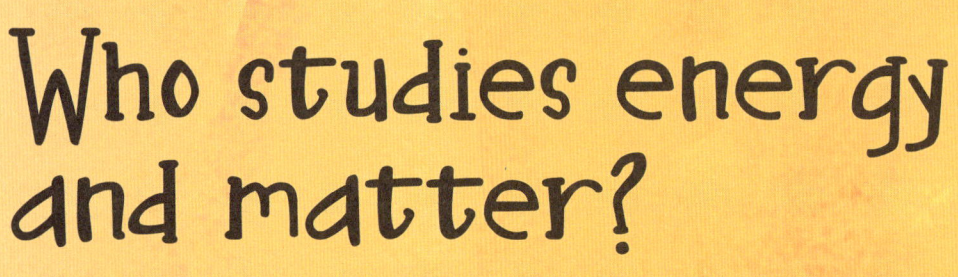

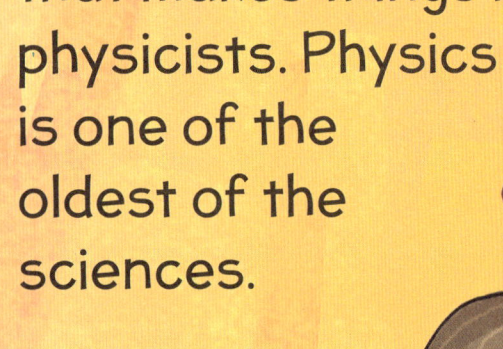

I discovered the radioactive elements radium and polonium.

Who investigated radioactivity?

Marie Curie was a famous scientist who studied a mysterious energy called radioactivity. Along with her husband Pierre, she discovered two new elements in 1898.

How did X-rays help?

Marie Curie also invented a mobile X-ray machine to help treat wounded soldiers in World War 1. It could be driven to the battlefield and allowed doctors to see inside the bodies of patients.

Marie and her daughter, Irene, trained women volunteers as X-ray operators.

Who saw the light?

Albert Einstein was a genius. He worked out that nothing can travel faster than light. He showed that time and space could change, depending on how fast you were going when you measured them! Einstein changed the way we think about the Universe.

This is my most famous equation!

$$E=mc^2$$

Who is looking into the atom?

As well as being famous for his television programmes explaining science, **Professor Brian Cox** also carries out important research into what makes up atoms, the tiny building blocks of matter.

What are things made of?

Chemistry is all about substances, called chemicals, that everything, including us, is made of. Scientists who study what happens when different chemicals mix together are called chemists.

The shape shown in Photo 51 proved that DNA has a twisted ladder-like structure.

Photo 51 revealed what DNA actually looks like.

Who took Photo 51?

Rosalind Franklin's X-ray photographs in 1952 helped to discover the structure of DNA. DNA is like an information store in all living things that determines how they look and function.

Did you know?

As well as being a great physicist, **Galileo** also discovered the four largest moons of the planet Jupiter.

Callisto, Ganymede, Europa and Io are known as the Galilean moons!

Galileo discovered the moons with a telescope he built himself.

Isaac Newton's three laws of motion describe how everything in the Universe moves, from tennis balls to stars.

The Sun is at the centre of the Solar System, not us!

People used to think that the Sun went around the Earth until, in the 1500s, **Nicolaus Copernicus** explained that Earth and the other planets go around the Sun.

X-rays were discovered accidentally by German physicist **Wilhelm Röentgen** in 1895.

In the 1860s British doctor **Joseph Lister** showed that simple hygiene like washing your hands can help prevent diseases spreading.

French chemist **Louis Pasteur** proved that bacteria can be the cause of harmful diseases.

Ada Lovelace Day is held each year to celebrate women in STEM.

The very first computer program was written by **Ada Lovelace** more than 150 years ago!

The Nobel Prize is awarded for great scientific discoveries. **Marie Curie** is one of only five people to have won it twice!

I won for Physics in 1903 and Chemistry in 1911.

Who found life in a drop of water?

About 300 years ago, **Antonie van Leeuwenhoek** from Holland made microscopes that allowed him to see tiny living things swimming in a drop of water. These little microbes were too small to see normally.

I'm a microbiologist. I study very tiny living things.

I'm an entomologist. I study insects.

Can bees tell the time?

In 1929, German biologist **Ingeborg Beling** trained bees to come to a feeding station at the same time every day. She discovered that bees have a built in 'biological clock' that tells them what time of day it is.

I'm also a scientist of agriculture (farming).

How many things can you do with a peanut?

African-American botanist **George Washington Carver** developed around 300 products made from peanuts in the early 20th century, including flour, paper and soap.

I also studied coprolites — fossilized poo!

In 1823, Mary discovered the first complete skeleton of a plesiosaur, a long-necked marine reptile.

Who looks back in time?

Planet Earth, and the plants and animals that live on it, have not always been the same. Geologists study the way the Earth changes and palaeontologists find out about life long ago.

Who found a strange monster?

Mary Anning was one of the first people to study life from long ago. When she was just 12, Mary found the body of an ichthyosaur, an extinct reptile that lived in the sea over 190 million years ago. Her brother found the skull!

Who is looking out in space?

Scientists who study the planets, stars and other objects in space are called astronomers. Space scientists design spacecraft to explore far beyond the Earth.

Comet

Pulsar

At first, it was thought that the pulsars' signals could be coming from alien 'little green men'!

Can you spot a comet?
Caroline Herschel was a talented astronomer. She discovered objects in space that no one had seen before, including eight comets.

I helped to build the huge radio telescope that picked up signals of pulsars!

There is a huge black hole at the centre of the Milky Way!

Caroline Herschel

Jocelyn Bell Burnell

Stephen Hawking

If a comet flies near the Sun, gas and dust stream away from its core, forming shining tails.

Black hole

What happens inside a black hole?

Nobody really knows! A black hole has such an immense pull of gravity that nothing can escape it, not even light. **Professor Stephen Hawking** was one of the world's greatest experts on these mysterious objects.

Who discovered pulsars?

Pulsars are unusual stars that spin very quickly and give out pulses of high-energy radiation. They were discovered by **Jocelyn Bell Burnell** in 1967, when she was just 24 years old.

Andromeda galaxy

Hubble Space Telescope

Edwin Hubble

How big is space?

Space is very big — and it is getting bigger! Astronomer **Edwin Hubble** discovered that the Universe is expanding like a huge balloon.

The Hubble Space Telescope was named after me!

127

Who knows how the human body works?

Medical scientists have made amazing breakthroughs in understanding the human body, and why problems sometimes happen.

What's that smell?

Humans can pick out a trillion different scents. Scientists **Linda Buck** and **Richard Axel** discovered how the nose and the brain work together in the sense of smell.

Cells

Smell particles

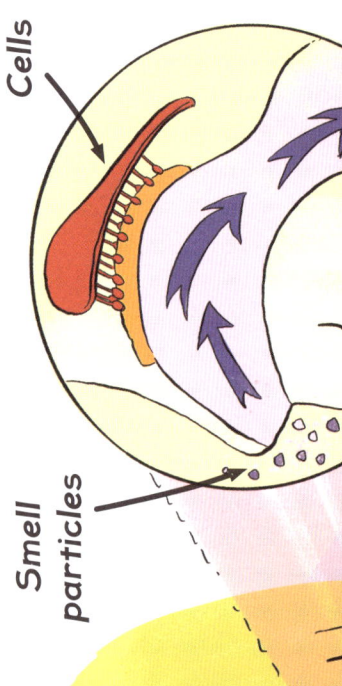

Smell particles are detected by tiny cells in your nose, which then send signals to your brain.

Everything you do, think and say is controlled by your brain.

What's going on inside your head?

Neuroscientists study our brain and nervous system. **Padma Srivastava** pioneers treatments for serious conditions.

Can scientists save the planet?

Climate change is something that concerns all of us. Environmental scientists can help us find ways of tackling the problem.

Through the work of scientists, we now know that climate change makes wildfires and storms more likely.

What's happening to the climate?

Climatologist **James Hansen** was one of the first scientists to show how changes in the atmosphere are causing the Earth's temperature to increase, changing the climate.

What can we do to help?

Environmentalists like **Wangari Maathai** in Africa lead the way in the fight for the environment. She started the Green Belt Movement, aiming to plant millions of trees to replace those that have been lost.

You could be an environmentalist too!

What's happening in the ocean?

Changes aren't just happening in the air and on the land. Marine biologists like **Sylvia Earle** are showing what a terrible effect climate change is having on ocean life as well.

I'm a marine biologist. I study life in the ocean.

Can we travel in time?

Some scientists think that it might be possible, but it would be very, very difficult and beyond what we can do at the moment.

I don't have time for this!

I might need a bigger cake!

Is it possible to live forever?

Scientists are looking into ways to slow down the process of ageing. So we might live longer, but perhaps not forever.

How many different living things are there?

Nobody knows for sure. So far scientists have named 1.2 million different species (kinds) of plants and animals, but there could be as many as 10 million that we haven't named yet.

Some species may go extinct before they're even discovered.

Why do we yawn?

Surprisingly, scientists are still puzzling over that one. Perhaps it helps get more blood to the brain to make us more alert, but we're just not sure!

index

A
Aboriginal peoples 25, 27
Aderin-Pocock, Maggie 115
Admiralty Island 17
Africa 28–29
Age of Exploration 20–21
ageing process 135
Al-Jazari, Ismail 83
Aldrin, Buzz 37
Amazon rainforest 63, 72
Amazon River 45, 48
Amos, Ruth 101
Amundsen, Roald 32, 33
Analytical Engine 94
Angel Falls 67
Anning, Mary 124
Antarctica 38, 54–55
Apollo missions 37, 57, 68–69
aquariums 104
Archimedes 83, 111
Armstrong, Neil 37
astronauts/cosmonauts 36–37, 40, 51, 57, 68–69, 71, 113
astronomers 108, 114, 120, 126–127
atoms 117
Attenborough, David 115
Australia 25, 27, 41

B
Babbage, Charles 94
bacteria 90, 115, 121
Baird, John Logie 81
Banerjee, Shubham 101
Banks, Joseph 24
Baret, Jeanne 25
batteries 88
Battles, Ashley 51
bees 123
Bell, Alexander Graham 89
Bell Burnell, Jocelyn 126, 127
Bell, Gertrude 17
Benz, Bertha 45
Benz, Karl 45, 85
Berners-Lee, Tim 95, 115
bicycles 44, 76–77, 92
Bingham, Hiram 16
biologists 122–123, 133
Bird, Isabella 16
Bíró, László 103
black holes 126, 127
Blanchard, Sophie 59
blood circulation 131
Bluetooth 95, 102
Bly, Nellie 22, 46
bomb code-breaking machine 80
book production 79
botanists 24, 25, 122, 123
Braille printer 101
brain 130
Braun, Wernher von 84
breakfast cereals 92, 97
Bungaree 25
Burke, Robert 27
Burton, Richard 28
buses, double-decker 85
Bushnell, Nolan 103

C
camels 27
Canada 21
cars 45, 56, 85
Carson, Rachel 114
Cartier, Jacques 21
Carver, George Washington 123
cat's eyes 104
caving 50
Challenger Deep 71
chemical elements 119
chemists 108, 114, 118–119, 121
child inventors 100–101
circumnavigation of the world 20, 22, 39, 44, 46–47, 56, 58
Clark, William 26
climate change 132–133
climatologists 132
Coca Cola 80
Cochran, Josephine 80
code-breaking 80
Collins, Michael 37
Columbus, Christopher 19
comets 126
computers 86, 94–95, 115, 121
Concorde jet 47
conservationists 122
Cook, Frederick 32
Cook, James 24
Copernicus, Nicolaus 120
coprolites 124
Cosmic Time 81
Cousteau, Jacques and Simone 35
Covid-19 pandemic 90, 109
Cox, Brian 117
Cray, Seymour 95
Crayola crayons 86
Crusoe, Robinson 73
cuneiform writing 79
Curie, Marie and Pierre 116–117, 121

D
Darwin, Charles 60–61, 125
Davy, Humphry 88
Defoe, Daniel 73
Denali 45
denim jeans 81
dinosaurs 125
Disappointment, Mount 17
dishwashers 80
DNA 118
Drake, Francis 22
dynamite 87
Dyson, James 86

E
e-readers 79
Earhart, Amelia 66
Earth, weight of 114
earthquake detector 83
Edison, Thomas 86, 89
Egyptians, ancient 12, 79
Einstein, Albert 117
Elcano, Juan Sebastián 20
electricity 88–89
emojis 80
English Channel 67
entomologists 63, 123
environmental movement 114, 115, 132–133
Eratosthenes 110, 111
Erik the Red 18
Everest, Mount 23, 34
evolution 60, 125
extinction 137

F
Faraday, Michael 88
Fawcett, Percy 72
Fiennes, Ranulph 39
Flinders, Matthew 25
Ford Model T 56
fossils 124, 125
Franklin, Benjamin 88
Franklin, Rosalind 118

G
Gagarin, Yuri 36
Galápagos Islands 60, 125
Galileo Galilei 113, 120
Gama, Vasco da 20
Gates, Bill 87
generators 88
geologists 124, 128
Gilbert, Sarah 109
Goddard, Robert 84
gold 22
Goodall, Jane 122
Gotthard Base Tunnel 70
Grand Canyon 48, 65
gravity 112, 113, 127
Great Pacific Garbage Patch 98
Greeks, ancient 79, 110–111
Green Belt Movement 133
Greenland 18, 19
Gutenberg, Johannes 79

H
Haartsen, Jaap 102
Hansen, James 132
Harald Bluetooth 102
Harvey, William 131
Hatshepsut, Queen 12
Hawking, Stephen 126, 127
Henson, Matthew 32
Herbert, Wally 33
Herschel, Caroline 126
Heyerdahl, Thor 52–53
hieroglyphs 79
Hillary, Edmund 23, 34
Horie, Kenichi 50
hot-air balloons 57, 58–59, 65
hoverboards 67
HTML 95
Hubble Space Telescope 127
human body 130–131
Humboldt, Alexander von 62

I
Ibn Battuta 15
ice cream 14
Inca 16
International Space Station 47, 113
IV backpacks 101

J
Jefferson, Thomas 26
Jemison, Mae 40
Jenner, Edward 109
Johnson, Amy 23
Johnson, Lonnie 96, 97
junks (trading ships) 15

K
Kaufmann, Elsie Effah 131
Kellogg brothers 92, 97
Kevlar 119
Kingsley, Mary 17, 49, 65
Knight, Margaret 76
Kon-Tiki expedition 53
Kurita, Shigetaka 80
Kurup, Deepika 99
Kwolek, Stephanie 119

L
Lamarr, Hedy 95
laws of motion 120
Leeuwenhoek, Antonie van 115, 123
LEGO 105
Leif Erikson 19
Leonardo da Vinci 82–83, 87
Lewis, Meriwether 26
life on other planets 134
Lion Lights 100
Lister, Joseph 121
Livingstone, David 29, 38
Lovelace, Ada 94, 121

M
Maathai, Wangari 133
McCandless, Bruce 51
McDouall Stuart, John 27
Machu Picchu 16
Magellan, Ferdinand 20, 21, 47, 52
Magie, Lizzie J 86
Makosinski, Ann 101
Marcet, Jane 114
Mariana Trench 35
marine biologists 133
Mars 41, 64
mathematicians 94, 111
mechanical toys 83
medicine 90–91, 109, 121
Mendeleev, Dmitri 119
Merian, Maria Sibylla 63
Mestral, George de 102
metamorphosis 63
microbiology 90, 123, 129
microplastic particles 99
microscopes 90, 115, 123
Milky Way 114, 126
Minecraft 92
mirror writing 83
mirrors 78
mobile phones 89
Monopoly 86
Moon landings 22, 37
Morse Code 89

N
NASA 22, 84
Native Americans 21, 26, 52, 53
neuroscientists 130
Newton, Isaac 112, 120
Niagara Falls 49, 65
Nile, River 28, 29
Nissen, George 87
Nobel, Alfred 87
Nobel Prize 87, 121
North Pole 32–33, 45

O
Ocean Cleanup system 98
ocean rowing 51
ornithologists 129
Osterud, Joann 70
Ottoman Empire 17
Outen, Sarah 51

P
Pacific Islanders 52
Pacific Ocean 13, 21, 26, 51, 52–53
Padalka, Gennady 57
palaeontologists 124, 125
pandemics 90, 109
parachuting 64
Pasteur, Louis 121
Peary, Jo 33
Peary, Robert 32, 33
Peck, Annie Smith 16

Pemberton, John 80
penny farthing bicycles 77, 92
Periodic Table 119
Persson, Markus 92
Pfeiffer, Isa 23
Phillips, Van 90
Phoenicians 79
physicists 116–117, 121
Piccard, Jacques 35
planes 22, 23, 47, 51, 56, 66–67, 70, 82, 84
PlanetSolar 85
plaster casts 91
plastic pollution 98, 99
Play-Doh 81
Polo, Marco 14, 16
polonium 116
Polynesians 13, 52, 53
Pong 103
post-it notes 97
Powell, John Wesley 48
power plants 89
printing presses 79
prosthetics 90, 131
pulsars 126, 127
Pytheas 13, 73

R
radioactivity 116
radium 116
rainforests 53, 64, 72
Rivera, Gadiel Sanchez 63
robots 93
Rocket steam locomotive 87
rockets 84
Romans 79
Röntgen, Wilhelm 91, 121
Roosevelt, Theodore 81
Rutherford, Zara 56

S
Sacagawea 26
Saturn V rockets 84
scientific method 109
scientists 106–137
Scott, Robert Falcon 33
scuba diving 35
Searle, Frank 85
Selkirk, Alexander 73
Seven Summits 34
Shackleton, Ernest 38, 54–55, 65
Shaw, Percy 104

Shima, Hideo 87
Shinkansen bullet trains 87
ships and boats 15, 24, 50, 51, 52, 85
silicon chips 94
Silk Road 14
Simonds, Kylie 101
Singhania, Vijaypat 58
slave trade 21
sleep 134
Slinky toys 96
smallpox 109
smell, sense of 130
solar cells 99
solar power 84, 85
Solar System 23, 120
South Pole 64
space exploration 23, 36–37, 40, 41, 51, 57, 68–9, 126–127
species, number of 137
Speke, John 28
Spiers, Reg 50
Spotts, Woni 57
Srivastava, Padma 130
Stafford, Ed 63
StairSteady 101
Stanley, Henry 29
Stark, Freya 39
stars 114, 127
steam locomotives 87
Stephenson, George 87
Stevens, Thomas 44
sticking plasters 91
Strauss, Levi 81
Strel, Martin 48
submarines 51
submersibles 35, 71
Sullivan, Kathy 71
Sumerians 79

T
Tabei, Junko 34
tanks, battle 82
Tasman, Abel 41
Taylor, Annie Edson 49
teddy bears 81
telephones 89
telescopes 120, 126, 127
television 81
Tenzing Norgay 23, 34
Tereshkova, Valentina 36
Thales 110
Thor, Mount 50

time travel 135
Tinné, Alexine 29
trade routes 14, 20
trains 50, 56, 87
trampolines 87
Turere, Richard 100
Turing, Alan 80

U
Uemura, Naomi 45
underwater exploration 35
unicycles 77

V
vaccines 90, 109
Valley of the Assassins 39
Velcro 102
Victoria Falls 29
Victoria, Lake 28
video games 92, 103
Viellepreux-Power, Jeanne 104
Vikings 18, 51
Vinland 19
Volta, Alessandro 88

W
Walsh, Don 35
Wanderwell, Aloha 56
water purification 99
Watson, Thomas 89
Wifi 95
Wills, William 27
World Wide Web 95, 115
Wright, Orville and Wilbur 22, 84
writing systems 79

X Y
X-rays 91, 117, 118, 121, 131
Yamazaki, Shunpei 115

Z
Zhang Heng 83
Zheng He 15
zoologists 108, 122